Congressional
Research
Service

Improper Payments and Recovery Audits: Legislation, Implementation, and Analysis

Garrett Hatch
Specialist in American National Government

Meredith A. Levine
Analyst in Government Organization and Management

January 2, 2013

Congressional Research Service

7-5700

www.crs.gov

R42878

Summary

As Congress searches for ways to generate savings, reduce the deficit, and fund federal programs, it has held hearings and passed legislation to prevent and recover improper payments. Improper payments—which exceeded $115 billion in FY2011—are payments made in an incorrect amount, payments that should not have been made at all, or payments made to an ineligible recipient or for an ineligible purpose. The total amount of improper payments may be even higher than reported because several agencies have yet to determine improper payment amounts for many programs, including some with billions of dollars in annual expenditures.

In 2002, Congress passed the Improper Payments Information Act (IPIA, P.L. 107-300; 116 Stat. 2350), which established an initial framework for identifying, measuring, preventing, and reporting on improper payments at each agency. That same year, Congress also passed legislation, the Recovery Audit Act (P.L. 107-107; Section 831; 115 Stat. 1186), which required agencies that awarded more than $500 million annually in contracts to establish programs to recover overpayments to contractors.

After five years of reporting, the data indicated that while many individual programs reduced their improper payment rates, the total amount of improper payments and the government-wide improper payment rate both increased. Since the IPIA reporting requirements took effect, agencies have expanded the number of programs reported each year. One potential consequence of this expansion is that the annual dollar amount of improper payments reported has more than doubled over time from $45 billion in FY2004 to $115 billion in FY2011.

In response, Congress passed new legislation, the Improper Payments Elimination and Recovery Act of 2010 (IPERA, P.L. 111-204; 124 Stat. 2224), which replaced and consolidated the requirements of both IPIA and the Recovery Audit Act. IPERA retained the core provisions of the IPIA while requiring improvements in agency improper payment estimation methodologies and improper payment reduction plans. It also significantly expanded the scope and reporting requirements of recovery audit programs.

This report examines the key provisions of IPERA and analyzes its effectiveness at reducing improper payments and increasing payment recoveries. IPERA may have had a positive impact on efforts to recoup overpayments—agencies recaptured more than $1.2 billion in improper payments in FY2011, which is nearly double that recaptured in FY2010.

Legislation introduced in the 112th Congress would address some of the weaknesses in agency improper payment prevention controls and recovery audit programs. S. 1409, the Improper Payments Elimination and Recovery Improvement Act, passed the Senate with an amendment by unanimous consent in August 2012 and was then sent to the House and referred to the Committee on Oversight and Government Reform. The House passed a companion version of the bill, H.R. 4053, the Improper Payments Elimination and Recovery Improvement Act of 2012, on December 13, 2012, by a vote of 402-0. This report will be updated as necessary.

Contents

Tables

Contacts

Improper Payments and Audit Recovery Legislation

Overview

In an effort to reduce and ultimately eliminate billions of dollars in improper payments made by federal agencies each fiscal year, Congress passed the Improper Payments Information Act (IPIA, P.L. 107-300; 116 Stat. 2350) in 2002. IPIA established an initial framework for identifying, measuring, preventing, and reporting on improper payments at each agency. Separately, Congress also passed legislation, the Recovery Audit Act of 2002 (P.L. 107-107; Section 831; 115 Stat. 1186), which required agencies that awarded more than $500 million annually in contracts to implement plans to recover overpayments to contractors.[1]

Reports on improper payments and recovery audits were first issued for FY2004. After five years of reporting, the data showed that progress under IPIA was uneven—while many individual programs reduced their improper payment rates, the total amount of improper payments and the government-wide improper payment rate both increased between FY2004 and FY2008. During that same time period, Government Accountability Office (GAO) auditors had identified weaknesses in numerous agencies' recovery audit programs.[2]

In response, Congress passed new legislation, the Improper Payments Elimination and Recovery Act of 2010 (IPERA, P.L. 111-204; 124 Stat. 2224), which replaced and consolidated the requirements of both IPIA and the Recovery Audit Act. As discussed below, IPERA retained the core provisions of the IPIA while requiring improvements in agency improper payment estimation methodologies and improper payment reduction plans. It also significantly expanded the scope and reporting requirements of recovery audit programs.

Improper Payments

IPERA defines an improper payment as a payment that should not have been made or that was made in an incorrect amount, including both overpayments and underpayments. This definition includes payments that were made to an ineligible recipient, duplicate payments, payments for a good or service not received, and payments that do not account for credit for applicable discounts. Under IPERA, "payment" is defined as a transfer or commitment to transfer federal funds in the future—including cash, securities, loans, loan guarantees, and insurance subsidies—to a non-federal entity. Thus, the law applies to federal funds paid or obligated by a federal agency to non-federal grantees, contractors, and loan recipients, including state or local governments who administer federal programs or activities.

---

[1] P.L. 107-107 is the National Defense Authorization Act of FY2002. Section 831 of P.L. 107-107 is commonly referred to as the Recovery Audit Act of 2002.

[2] Government Accountability Office, *Status of Agencies' Efforts to Address Improper Payment and Recovery Auditing Requirements*, GAO-08-438T, January 31, 2008.

Risk Assessments

IPERA requires agencies to take specific steps to identify and reduce improper payments. First, it requires agencies to perform a risk assessment of all programs and activities and identify those that were susceptible to "significant" improper payments. IPERA defines "significant" for FY2011 and FY2012 as either (1) improper payments that exceed both $10 million and 2.5% of program or activity outlays; or (2) improper payments in excess of $100 million. Beginning in FY2013, the 2.5% threshold drops to 1.5%, with other aspects of the definition unchanged. IPERA also requires agencies to perform the initial risk assessment for every program and activity during the year in which IPERA was enacted (i.e., in 2011) and to perform subsequent risk assessments at least every three years.

When performing risk assessments, IPERA requires agencies to consider several risk factors that may make a program or activity susceptible to "significant" improper payments:

- whether the program or activity is new to the agency;

- the complexity of the program or activity;

- the volume of payments;

- whether payments or payment eligibility decisions are made outside the agency, such as by a state government;

- recent major changes in program funding, authorities, practices, or procedures;

- the level of experience and quality of training for personnel responsible for making program eligibility determinations or certifying that payments are accurate; and

- major deficiencies in an agency's audit report or other source that might result in inaccurate payment certification.

Once a program or activity has been identified as susceptible to "significant" improper payments, agencies are required to estimate the amount of improper payments made under each.

Reporting on Agency Efforts to Reduce Improper Payments

IPERA requires agencies to report on the actions they have taken to reduce improper payments for each program and activity in the accompanying materials to their annual financial statement. IPERA also requires agencies to provide an estimate of improper payments for each program or activity identified as susceptible through the risk assessment, describe the causes of improper payments, the actions planned or taken to correct those problems, and when those actions were completed or will be completed. Target dates for achieving reductions in improper payments must be approved by the Office of Management and Budget (OMB), and agencies must include annual performance criteria used to hold the appropriate parties accountable for meeting those targets—whether they work for the agency or for a state or local government that helps implement the program. The performance criteria must also include an evaluation of the internal controls within the agency, or state or local government, that are intended to prevent, detect, and recover improper payments. IPERA also requires agencies to include a statement as to whether they have sufficient resources to develop their own internal controls for reducing improper payments—such as human capital and information systems—and, if not, to identify what additional resources are needed to do so. OMB is also required to establish criteria that agencies must meet to demonstrate that they have effective internal control systems.

IPERA also requires OMB to submit a report to two congressional committees—the House Committee on Oversight and Government Reform and the Senate Committee on Homeland Security and Government Affairs—that provides a government-wide summary of agency efforts to reduce and recover improper payments. This report must include (1) government-wide improper payment reduction targets; (2) the compliance status of each agency; (3) a discussion of progress made towards meeting improper payment reduction targets; and (4) a summary of the improper payment reduction and recovery actions of each agency. IPERA further directs OMB to provide guidance on the timing and format of the improper payments reports required by IPERA, both at the agency level and government wide. OMB's guidance, which was issued in 2011, is discussed in detail in the "OMB Guidance" section of this report.

Compliance

The inspector general of each agency must determine whether the agency is in compliance with IPERA and report its findings to the head of the agency, the Comptroller General, the House Committee on Oversight and Government Reform, and the Senate Committee on Homeland Security and Government Affairs. An agency is deemed in compliance if it has

- published an annual financial statement;

- conducted risk assessments for each program or activity;

- published improper payment estimates, corrective action plans, and improper payment reduction targets for all risk-susceptible programs and activities; and

- reported no improper payment rate that met or exceeded 10%.

By definition, then, an agency must report that all of its programs and activities have an improper payment rate of less than 10% to be deemed in compliance with IPERA.

Agencies that are deemed non-compliant must submit a plan to Congress that describes the steps they will take to become fully compliant. The plan must include (1) measurable milestones that will result in compliance for each program or activity deemed non-compliant; (2) the name of a senior agency official who is responsible for ensuring the agency becomes compliant; and (3) an "accountability mechanism" that may include incentives and consequences tied to the ability of the responsible official to bring the agency into compliance.

If an agency is deemed non-compliant for two consecutive years, and OMB has determined that additional funding would help the agency become compliant, then the agency head would be required to obligate additional funds—in an amount determined by OMB—for "intensified compliance efforts." IPERA does not provide agencies with new authority for transferring funds. Agencies that were unable to obligate all of the additional funds required by OMB under their existing authorities, then, would need statutory authority to transfer funds under Title 31 of the *U.S. Code*.[3]

---

[3] 31 U.S.C. §1532.

If an agency is deemed non-compliant for three or more consecutive years for the same program or activity, then the agency must submit to Congress reauthorization proposals for those programs or activities, along with proposed statutory changes that may bring the agency into compliance.

IPERA gives OMB the authority to conduct compliance pilot programs to "test potential accountability mechanisms" and to report the findings from those pilot programs within five years from enactment (i.e., before July 22, 2015).

Recovery Audits

A recovery audit, or payment recapture audit, is a review process designed to identify overpayments. According to OMB guidance,[4] "It is not an audit in the traditional sense. Rather it is a detective and corrective control activity designed to identify and recapture overpayments, and, as such, is a management function and responsibility."[5]

The idea of recouping overpayments through the recovery auditing process had received attention in previous Congresses. In a hearing on eliminating agency payment errors, Senator Tom Carper[6] noted that, "even as agencies report greater improper payments, we are seeing actually fewer improper payments recovered."[7] When Senator Carper introduced IPERA in the 110th Congress, the legislation addressed this issue through the inclusion of a section on recovery audits.

IPERA requires agencies to perform recovery audits on each program or activity[8] with expenditures of $1 million or more per year. In addition, the legislation stipulates that the performance of recovery audits is conditional on cost-effectiveness, though the term "cost-effective" is not defined in law. IPERA contains provisions for the conduct of these recovery audits.[9] The legislation establishes agencies' threshold requirement for recovery auditing, details certain procedures for the performance of recovery audits, mandates collection of overpayments, specifies disposition allotments for recovered amounts, and imposes reporting requirements on actions to recover improper payments.

The legislation institutes two procedural requirements for the conduct of recovery audits. First, it requires agencies to prioritize both the most recent payments and those deemed susceptible to "significant" improper payments. Second, the legislation specifies options for recovery audit services—they could be performed within the agency itself or by other U.S. departments and agencies, or private sector services could be procured by contract.

---

[4] IPERA does not define the term "recovery audit."

[5] Office of Management and Budget, *OMB Circular A-123, Appendix C (Revised)*, April 14, 2011, at http://www.whitehouse.gov/sites/default/files/omb/memoranda/2011/m11-16.pdf.

[6] In the 112th Congress, Senator Tom Carper is the chairman of the Senate Subcommittee on Federal Financial Management, Government Information, Federal Services, and International Security, which held this hearing.

[7] U.S. Congress, Senate Committee on Homeland Security and Governmental Affairs, Subcommittee on Federal Financial Management, Government Information, Federal Services, and International Security, *Eliminating Agency Payment Errors*, 110th Cong., 2nd sess., January 31, 2008, S. Hrg. 110-501 (Washington: GPO, 2008), p. 4.

[8] IPERA does not provide a definition for "program" or "activity." OMB guidance on the implementation of IPERA states that "program and activity" is referred to as "program," and programs include grants, benefits, loans, and contract programs. See Office of Management and Budget, *OMB Circular A-123, Appendix C (Revised)*, April 14, 2011, at http://www.whitehouse.gov/sites/default/files/omb/memoranda/2011/m11-16.pdf.

[9] This law repealed that which established initial recovery audit requirements (P.L. 107-107).

Although IPERA permits contractors to conduct recovery audits on agencies' behalf, it circumscribes their scope of authority. Only with the express consent of the agency head are contractors authorized to notify entities of potential overpayments,[10] respond to questions pertaining to potential overpayments, and take administrative action on overpayment claims. In addition, contractors are not allowed to render a final decision as to whether or not an overpayment occurred, and they are not authorized to adjudicate overpayment claims. IPERA requires recovery audit contractors to report all overpayments detected through recovery audits to the procuring agency, regardless of whether a given overpayment occurred at the agency that contracted the audit or another agency beyond the scope of the contract.

Nongovernmental entities are prohibited from disclosing information uncovered through a recovery audit that would identify an individual for any purpose other than the recovery audit itself. An individual could waive this privacy protection, however, and permit the executive agency that contracted the audit to disclose identifying information for other purposes.

The legislation directs agencies to take "prompt and appropriate action" to collect overpayments identified in recovery audits upon receipt of an overpayment notification. Distribution of collected amounts was left to the discretion of agency heads, though there were limits on the maximum percentage of recovered amounts that could be applied to certain programs, purposes, and activities:

- At most, 25% for a financial management improvement program, to be implemented by agency heads to address improper payments and reduce errors and waste across agency programs and operations.

- At most, 25% credited to the appropriation or fund from which the overpayment was made.

- At most, 5% for inspector general activities relating to implementation of the legislation itself or investigation of improper payments.

- The remaining 45% of collected amounts—and up to 100% depending on how much the agencies actually allocated in accordance with these criteria—are to be deposited in the Treasury as miscellaneous receipts.

IPERA specifies four reporting requirements which relate to the conduct of recovery audits. First, the legislation requires agency heads to provide a report on improper payment recovery actions, which is to include a statistically valid estimate of improper payments made by each program or activity, along with the following:

- a discussion of the methods used to recover overpayments;

- the amounts recovered, outstanding, and determined not to be collectable;

- a written justification explaining any uncollected amounts;

- an aging schedule of outstanding amounts;[11]

---

[10] Entities may include persons (IPERA at 124 Stat. 2229).

[11] The aging schedule of outstanding amounts shows the amount of overpayments that have been identified through a payment recapture audit program but not yet recovered. Aging typically begins at the time when an overpayment has been detected. For a table template, see Table 4 in Office of Management and Budget, *Financial Reporting Requirements*, August 3, 2012, p. 157, at http://www.whitehouse.gov/sites/default/files/omb/assets/omb/circulars/a136/ (continued...)

- a summary of the disposition of recovered amounts;

- a discussion of conditions giving rise to improper payments and how these are being resolved; and

- if an agency determined that a recovery audit was not cost-effective, then a justification as to why.[12]

Second, by November 1 of each year, agencies are required to submit a report to OMB and Congress on actions taken on those conditions that promote overpayments, as identified and reported by recovery audit contractors. Third, the Director of OMB must provide the Senate Committee on Homeland Security and Governmental Affairs and the House Committee on Oversight and Government Reform a government-wide report on agencies' reports of improper payments information and recovery actions, as well as the compliance status of each agency covered by the law. Lastly, within two years of IPERA's enactment, the Chief Financial Officers Council must conduct a study, in consultation with the Council of Inspectors General on Integrity and Efficiency and recovery audit experts, on the implementation of IPERA's recovery audit provisions, the costs and benefits of agency recovery audit activities, and, in particular, the effectiveness of service provision by private contractors, agency employees, cross-servicing from other agencies, or any combination of the three. A report on this study was to be submitted to the Senate Committee on Homeland Security and Governmental Affairs, the House Committee on Oversight and Government Reform, and the Comptroller General by July 22, 2012.[13]

OMB Guidance

OMB circulars operationalize implementation for agencies. Frequently, if legislation gives OMB discretion over administrative concerns, OMB details the legislation's procedural requirements and may impose its own additional requirements, provided that these do not contravene the enacted legislation. IPERA requires OMB to issue implementation guidance to agencies. This government-wide guidance was issued April 11, 2011, through the revision of Appendix C of OMB Circular A-123 (hereafter, A-123), *Management's Responsibility for Internal Control*.[14] Agencies were required to begin using the revised guidance for their FY2011 reporting.

Improper Payments

OMB's definition of an improper payment is consistent with IPERA's, though A-123 clarifies that when an agency does not have the documentation necessary to determine that a payment was

---

(...continued)

a136_revised_2012.pdf

[12] The legislation does not indicate where the report was to be submitted. In the section on reporting the statistically valid estimates, it states that these estimates should be included in the materials accompanying the annual financial statement of the agency. OMB guidance on the implementation of IPERA states that agencies must report annually on their payment recapture program in their Performance and Accountability Reports (PARs) and Agency Financial Reports (AFRs). See Office of Management and Budget, *OMB Circular A-123, Appendix C (Revised)*, April 14, 2011, at http://www.whitehouse.gov/sites/default/files/omb/memoranda/2011/m11-16.pdf.

[13] As of December 15, 2012, CRS could not locate this report.

[14] Office of Management and Budget, *Circular A-123, Management's Responsibility for Internal Control*, December 21, 2004, at http://www.whitehouse.gov/omb/circulars_a123_rev.

---

proper, it is to be considered improper. OMB's guidance also provides a definition for program, which IPERA does not.[15] According to A-123, a program includes all types of grants, procurements, and credit programs, as well as regulatory activities, research and development activities, and activities that agencies perform to support their programs. OMB's guidance specifies that payments to other agencies and to employees are not considered programs.

Risk Assessments

A-123, like IPERA, requires agencies to (1) review all programs and identify those susceptible to improper payments; (2) develop a valid estimate of the amount of improper payments for those programs identified as susceptible to "significant" improper payments; (3) implement a plan to reduce improper payments; and (4) report estimates of the annual amounts of improper payments and progress in reducing them. For each of those steps, discussed below, A-123 establishes a detailed process by which agencies are to fulfill their obligations under IPERA.

A-123 and IPERA both use the same definition of "significant" improper payments for agencies to follow when identifying programs susceptible to improper payments, including the use of a 2.5% threshold for FY2011 and FY2012, and a 1.5% threshold for FY2013 and beyond. The guidance and IPERA also identified the same risk factors that may indicate a program is susceptible to "significant" improper payments. OMB may determine on a case-by-case basis whether certain programs below the threshold may be required to have risk assessments performed.

Like IPERA, A-123 requires OMB to approve of agency sampling methodologies to ensure they accurately reflect the annual amount of improper payments. A-123 provides agencies with detailed explanations of steps they should take to establish valid methodologies, including sampling technique and size. OMB's guidance specifies that improper payment estimates should only include the erroneous amount. For example, if a payment of $50 was due, and the agency paid $60, then only the $10 above the correct amount would be counted in the improper payment total. Similarly, if the agency had paid $40 to a recipient that was supposed to receive $50, then only the $10 below the correct amount would be counted as improper. However, if a $100 payment was made without sufficient documentation to confirm that the payment was correct, the entire $100 would be included in the improper payment total. A-123 permits agencies to sample transactions at certain steps within the lifecycle of a payment rather than the entire payment process, if the agency believes that only those steps have the highest risk or have the greatest return on investment. For example, if an agency determines that a five-step payment has two high-risk steps, then it may sample, review, and report an estimate for just those two steps.

A-123 mirrors IPERA in that it requires each agency to develop a plan to reduce improper payments that includes three components: a description of the root causes of improper payments for each risk-susceptible program; OMB-approved improper payment reduction targets and a timeline within which those targets will be reached; and the steps taken to ensure that all of the parties involved—federal and non-federal—are held accountable. The guidance does not provide examples of accountability mechanisms, but it does require agencies to assess whether they or their partners have the necessary infrastructure (i.e., human capital, internal controls, information systems) to reduce improper payments. A-123, like IPERA, also requires agencies to identify any statutory or regulatory barriers to implementing their plans. However, A-123 permits agencies to

---

[15] OMB uses the term "program" to refer to both programs and activities in Appendix C of A-123.

request a waiver for this reporting for programs or activities that have been deemed not risk-susceptible for two consecutive years, an allowance which is not found in IPERA.

A-123 requires agencies to include an estimate of the annual amount of improper payments for all of their programs and activities, and it clarifies that the estimate is to include programs or activities with estimated improper payment totals below $10 million. Consistent with IPERA, OMB's guidance also requires agencies to publish a report each year that includes the improper payment estimate; narrative information on agency plans to prevent, detect, and recover improper payments; and what resources, if any, they lack to implement their plans.

Compliance

A-123 provides numerous examples of steps agencies should take to prevent, detect, and recapture improper payments. The guidance acknowledges that fully implementing long-term corrective actions may take several years, but that those actions should be intensified and expanded whenever possible. A-123 identifies best-practices that could be used by agencies to reduce and recover improper payments, including predictive modeling, forensic accounting, partnering with agency inspectors general to focus on fraud prevention, data mining, and training agency staff on tools to identify improper payments.

Recovery Audits

As noted, IPERA requires agencies that have programs or activities with expenditures of $1 million or more per fiscal year to conduct payment recapture audits. A-123 further requires agencies to implement payment recapture audit programs, which consist of overall plans for risk analysis, payment recapture audits, and recapture (recovery) activities.[16] While the agency head has discretion over the manner and combination of payment recapture activities, the cost-effectiveness mandate means that the benefits of the payment recapture audit program, such as recaptured amounts, should exceed the costs of implementation and oversight. Payment recapture activities should include a management improvement program to address problems with internal controls that contributed to those overpayments identified through implementation of a payment recapture program.

A-123's scope for payment recapture audit programs is consistent with IPERA, though A-123 provides greater specificity regarding the types of programs and activities which require recovery audits, including grants, benefits, loans, and contract programs. In addition, A-123 states that agencies

- must prioritize payment recapture audits for the most recent payments and those deemed susceptible to "significant" improper payments;

---

[16] Recapture activities are designed to identify and recover overpayments identified by a payment recapture audit or post-award audit. A post-award audit is defined in the guidance as a "post-award examination of the accounting and financial records of a payment recipient that is performed by an agency official, or an authorized representative of the agency official." A post-award audit differs from a payment recapture audit in that a post-award audit is conducted to assess compliance with the terms of an award or contract, whereas a recovery audit is intended to identify overpayments.

- must design the program so as to ensure the greatest financial benefit for the government;

- may exclude payments from recovery audit activities if payment recapture audits are not determined to be cost-effective;

- may permit payment recapture audit contractors to notify entities of potential overpayments, respond to questions about overpayments, and take administrative action on overpayment claims but cannot authorize these contractors to render a final decision as to whether or not an overpayment occurred nor to adjudicate overpayment claims; and

- must correct underpayments identified through the recovery audit process, as well as overpayments.[17]

IPERA requires agencies to perform recovery audits if doing so is cost-effective. According to A-123, agencies should consider the likelihood of overpayment recapture in determining whether a recapture audit is cost-effective. In making this determination, agencies may weigh (1) whether laws or regulations permit recovery; (2) whether the recipient of the overpayment is likely to have resources to repay overpayments from non-federal funds; (3) whether the evidence of overpayment is clear versus contestable; and (4) whether the overpayment is truly a recoverable improper payment rather than a payment with unsupported documentation.[18]

If an agency determines that a payment recapture audit program would not be cost-effective, then it must advise OMB and the agency's inspector general of this decision, along with the analysis it performed to reach that decision. OMB may review the analysis and instruct the agency to conduct a payment recapture audit program.

Agencies are required to establish annual payment recapture targets for their programs, which should vary in accordance with the different types of payments the agency makes, such as grants versus contracts. Targets are based on the rate of recovery, which the guidance defines as "the amount of improper payments recovered divided by the amount of improper payments identified." Agencies may set their own targets for OMB review and approval but must aim for annual recapture targets of at least 85% within three years.[19] If they cannot achieve this target by FY2013, they must provide OMB a justification for setting a lowered target and obtain OMB's approval before setting it.

A-123 establishes guidelines for coordination between federal agencies and state or local governments, with respect to both payment recapture audits and financial management improvement efforts authorized by IPERA. Grant programs are subject to IPERA's recovery audit provisions, as noted previously, and these programs are often administered by states and local governments. The guidance instructs federal agencies to work with state and local governments to ensure that sufficient resources are available to perform payment recapture audits; federal agencies must also coordinate among themselves to reach partnerships with grant recipients for cost-effective payment recapture audit implementation. In addition, agency heads are required to

---

[17] IPERA's recovery audit provisions are limited to overpayments.

[18] Agencies may also consider the likelihood that expected recoveries will exceed the costs associated with identifying overpayments. This hinges on the availability of tools that can efficiently perform the recovery audits and whether such tools can be employed to identify significant overpayments in lieu of labor-intensive techniques.

[19] The first reporting year is FY2011, the second is FY2012, and the third is FY2013.

---

use information obtained from payment recapture programs to implement financial management improvement programs that will improve the agency's internal controls to address improper payments, as well as reduce errors and waste across agency programs and operations. In so doing, agencies with state-administered programs may provide money to states and local governments for their financial management improvement efforts.[20]

IPERA specifies three options for recovery audit services—recovery audits can be performed (1) within the agency itself, (2) by other U.S. departments and agencies, or (3) by a private sector entity. A-123 added a fourth option: by non-federal entities that expend federal awards.[21] IPERA allows agencies flexibility in the type of contract they use to procure recovery audit services, including contingency contracts, in which private sector contractors receive a percentage of overpayments that the agency is able to collect as payment for their services.[22] However, certain types of payments recovered—amounts recovered due to interim improper payments made under ongoing contracts, recoveries from non-discretionary appropriations, amounts recovered from unexpired appropriations, amongst others—cannot be used to pay contingency fee contracts. In these cases, agencies must establish alternative payment arrangements, such as through appropriations, to pay contractors.

A specific set of requirements and prohibitions governs the use of contracted payment recapture auditing firms. Contractors are required to provide semi-annual reports to the contracting agency on conditions giving rise to improper payments and recommendations for mitigation of these conditions; notify the agency of identified overpayments, regardless of whether they occurred at the contracting agency or another agency beyond the scope of the contract; and report credible evidence of fraud to the agency and its Office of Inspector General. In addition, contractors must familiarize themselves with agencies' policies and procedures and protect the confidentiality of sensitive financial information that could identify an individual. Payment recapture audit contractors are not prohibited from visiting the property of a payment recapture audit subject, though they cannot compel the production of records or information from the agency's contractors, nor can they act as agents for the federal government in the recovery of funds. Actual collection activities are carried out by federal agencies or non-federal entities expending federal awards; a payment recapture audit contractor may only perform the collection activity if it is permitted by statute.

A-123 elaborates on IPERA's delineation of the disposition of amounts from non-expired and expired discretionary funds. Overpayments recaptured from non-expired discretionary funds, appropriated after the enactment of IPERA, must be returned to the appropriation from which they were made and not used for any other purpose. Overpayments from mandatory fund accounts, trust fund accounts, or special fund accounts must revert back to those accounts, as well. The distribution of any expired, recaptured discretionary collected amounts is at the discretion of agency heads, though amounts allocated to (1) the financial management improvement program, (2) the appropriation or fund from which the overpayment was made, or (3) inspector general activities are subject to maximum limits under IPERA. Within these

---

[20] Under IPERA, up to 25 percent of funds recovered through a payment recapture audit program may be dedicated to financial management improvement programs, a portion of which may be distributed to state and local governments for these purposes.

[21] A non-federal entity is a state, local government, or non-profit organization. Defined in Office of Management and Budget, *OMB Circular A-133: Audits of States, Local Governments, and Non-Profit Organizations*, June 30, 1997, at http://www.whitehouse.gov/sites/default/files/omb/assets/a133/a133_revised_2007.pdf.

[22] Under these contracts, recoveries must be collected by the agency before payments to contractors are rendered.

constraints, agency heads may determine the actual percentages after reimbursing expenses for administering payment recapture audit programs and paying contractors for payment recapture audit services.

IPERA subjects agencies to two reporting requirements. First, it requires agencies to report annually on their payment recapture audit programs in their Performance and Accountability Reports (PARs) or Agency Financial Reports (AFRs). OMB's guidance on information to be included in these reports is consistent with IPERA, though it adds some additional requirements:[23]

- Provision of the total amount of payments subject to review, the actual amount of payments reviewed, the amounts identified for recapture, and the amounts actually recaptured in the current year; these amounts should be separated by those attributable to internal agency activities versus payment recapture audit contractors.

- Description and justification of the classes of payments excluded from payment recapture audit review by the agency.

Second, agencies using federal employees or external contractors must complete an additional annual report for OMB, Congress, and their inspectors general, containing recommendations from payment recapture auditors on mitigation of conditions that promote overpayments and corrective actions taken by the agency in response to these recommendations. It is due by November 1 each year and should describe recommendations and actions taken by the agency during the previous fiscal year.

Analysis

Agencies have had 10 years to implement improper payment legislation, beginning with the enactment of IPIA in 2002, which established the core requirements of improper payments reduction. IPERA, while enacted more recently, reinforced IPIA's core requirements and expanded agencies' responsibilities to prevent and recover improper payments. Therefore, it is possible to evaluate agency efforts in reducing payment error rates over several years, and to make an initial assessment of recovery audit programs.

Improper Payments: Limited Program

The government's improper payment rate has increased from approximately 4.4% in FY2004—the first year of reporting required by IPIA—to approximately 4.7% in FY2011, as shown in **Table 1**.[24] As a consequence, agencies continue to make tens of billions of dollars a year in improper payments. Since the IPIA reporting requirements took effect, agencies have made over

---

[23] This accompanies the requirement discussed previously in which the agency must advise OMB and the agency's Inspector General of the decision not to conduct a payment recapture audit if it would not be cost-effective. The PAR or AFR should contain a list of programs and activities for which a payment recapture audit was determined not to be cost-effective, and a description of the justifications and analysis used in making that determination.

[24] Office of Management and Budget, *Improper Payment Rates Across the Federal Government (FYs 2004-2011)*, PaymentAccuracy.gov, at http://paymentaccuracy.gov/tabular-data/govt-wide-improper-rates.

---

half a trillion dollars ($571 billion) in improper payments. In FY2011 alone the government made $115 billion in improper payments.[25]

The inability of the government to reduce its overall improper payment rate is partly due to agencies' failure to reduce substantially the error rates for risk-susceptible federal programs with multi-billion dollar annual outlays. In some cases, error rates for those programs have actually increased over time. Moreover, the full extent of the improper payment problem is not known because agencies have yet to develop improper payment rates for some programs, including programs which OMB estimates may have annual improper payments of at least $750 million annually.[26]

Table 1. Government-Wide Improper Payment Amounts and Rates (FY2004–FY2011)

($ amounts in billions)

	Improper Payment Amount ($)	Improper Payment Rate (%)
FY2004	45	4.35
FY2005	38	3.14
FY2006	41	2.91
FY2007	42	2.81
FY2008	73	3.95
FY2009	105	5.42
FY2010	121	5.29
FY2011	115	4.69

Source: Office of Federal Financial Management, Office of Management and Budget. *Improper Payments Dataset*, at http://www.whitehouse.gov/omb/financial/improper_payment_dataset.

Notes: Data in this table constructed from the Office of Federal Financial Management's improper payments dataset. Amounts and rates are approximate due to rounding.

Agencies did not have improper payment estimates in place for all of their risk-susceptible programs and activities for the first year of IPIA reporting, FY2004. Since then, agencies have expanded the number of programs reported each year as they develop valid improper payment estimates for them. As a consequence of this constant expansion, the annual dollar amount of improper payments reported has more than doubled over time, rising from $45 billion in FY2004 to $115 billion in FY2011.[27]

While the inclusion of additional programs accounts for much of the growth in improper payments reported since FY2004,[28] there are a number of multi-billion dollar programs which

---

[25] Office of Management and Budget, *Improper Payment Amounts Across the Federal Government (FYs 2004-2011)*, PaymentAccuracy.gov, at http://paymentaccuracy.gov/improper-payment-amounts.

[26] Office of Management and Budget, *Improper Payment Rates Across the Federal Government (FYs 2004-2011)*, PaymentAccuracy.gov, at http://paymentaccuracy.gov/content/programs-not-reported.

[27] Office of Management and Budget, *Improper Payment Amounts Across the Federal Government (FYs 2004-2011)*, PaymentAccuracy.gov, at http://paymentaccuracy.gov/improper-payment-amounts.

[28] GAO has attributed increases in aggregate improper payment amounts over time to newly reported programs or (continued...)

---

have seen little or no improvement in their improper payment rates, and in some cases the error rates for these programs have actually increased over time. The improper payment rate for the Medicare Fee-for-Service program, for example, increased from 5.2% in FY2005 to 8.6% in FY2011, and the amount of improper payments made under the program has more than doubled in that same period of time, increasing from $12 billion to $29 billion.[29] Similarly, the improper payment rate for the Unemployment Insurance (UI) program increased from 10% in FY2005 to 12% in FY2011, and the amount of improper payments under UI increased from $3 billion to $14 billion.[30] Error rates—and improper payment amounts—have also increased over time for the Supplemental Security Income program and Medicare Advantage (Part C).[31] While OMB has argued that administrative problems, such as the lack of required documentation, are the root causes of most improper payments,[32] this does not explain why a program's improper payment error rate would increase over time—particularly when agencies were to begin addressing these weaknesses 10 years ago with the enactment of IPIA.

Incomplete Scope

The full scope of improper payments has not been determined because agencies have not yet developed estimates for all of their risk-susceptible programs or are re-calculating their initial estimates. Among these programs are several that have multi-billion dollar outlays and may have annual improper payment amounts in the hundreds of millions to billions of dollars. The Department of Health and Human Services (HHS), for example, is re-estimating its error rate for the Children's Health Insurance Program (CHIP). In FY2008, HHS initially reported an error rate of 14.7% for CHIP and outlays of $5.7 billion, resulting in $834 million in improper payments.[33] Similarly, the Federal Communications Commission (FCC) is re-estimating the improper payment rate for the High-Cost Program component of the Universal Service Fund (USF). The initial improper payment rate for the High-Cost Program, published for FY2007 expenditures, was 16.5%, and total outlays exceeded $3.7 billion, resulting in $620 million in improper payments that year.[34] One of the largest risk-susceptible programs that lacks a valid improper payment error rate is the Earned Income Tax Credit (EITC), which is administered by the Department of the Treasury. The initial improper payment rate for the EITC, published for FY2004 expenditures, was 24.5%, with total outlays $39.4 billion, resulting in $9.7 billion in

---

(...continued)

increases in improper payments in specific programs. On newly reported programs, see Government Accountability Office, *Improper Payments: Agencies' Efforts to Address Improper Payment and Recovery Auditing Requirements Continue*, GAO- GAO-07-635T, March 2007, p. 8, at http://www.gao.gov/assets/120/116089.pdf. On increases in specific programs, see Government Accountability Office, *Improper Payments: Recent Efforts to Address Improper Payments and Remaining Challenges*, GAO-11-575, April 2011, p. 5, at http://www.gao.gov/new.items/d11575t.pdf.

[29] Office of Management and Budget, *Improper Payment Amounts Across the Federal Government (FYs 2004-2011)*, PaymentAccuracy.gov, at http://paymentaccuracy.gov/programs/medicare-fee-service.

[30] Office of Management and Budget, *Improper Payment Amounts Across the Federal Government (FYs 2004-2011)*, PaymentAccuracy.gov, at http://paymentaccuracy.gov/programs/unemployment-insurance.

[31] Office of Management and Budget, *Improper Payment Amounts Across the Federal Government (FYs 2004-2011)*, PaymentAccuracy.gov, at http://paymentaccuracy.gov/programs/medicare-advantage-part-c.

[32] Office of Management and Budget, *Improper Payment Amounts Across the Federal Government (FYs 2004-2011)*, PaymentAccuracy.gov, at http://paymentaccuracy.gov/about-improper-payments.

[33] Office of Management and Budget, *Improving the Accuracy and Integrity of Federal Payments*, January 8, 2009, p. 21, at http://www.whitehouse.gov/sites/default/files/omb/assets/about_omb/2008_ipia_final.pdf.

[34] Ibid., p. 23.

improper payments.[35] OMB estimates that the FY2011 improper payment rate for the EITC was between 21% and 26%, with a "rough" estimate of improper payments in excess of $15 billion.[36] Until these and all other risk-susceptible programs have valid improper payment rates, the extent of the problem will remain unknown.

Ineffective Internal Controls

According to GAO, many agencies have not yet established internal controls that are effective enough to significantly reduce the risk of improper payments.[37] As noted, OMB has reported that the three most common causes of improper payments are administrative in nature, specifically due to agencies failing to (1) verify that recipient-reported information is accurate, such as whether a recipient is working; (2) ensure that requests for payments are for valid purposes, such as whether a claim for a particular medical service is necessary given the recipient's medical condition; and (3) have the required documentation for each recipient, such as a completed application for benefits.

To address these deficiencies, GAO has recommended that agencies to consider implementing a range of preventive controls, including technological tools.[38] Among these tools, GAO recommended that agencies share data to validate recipient eligibility from a variety of sources. HHS, for example, shares information from its New Hires database with the Department of Labor to confirm the employment status of an individual claiming benefits from the Unemployment Insurance program.[39] GAO also recommended that agencies utilize predictive analytic technologies, which identify unusual patterns or abnormalities in service utilization or billing that may indicate fraudulent activity.[40] Predictive analytic technology, for example, is currently employed by HHS to screen all claims under the Medicare Fee-for-Service program prior to payment. GAO is evaluating the effectiveness of the technology in preventing payments for fraudulent claims.[41]

GAO also recommended that agencies provide more extensive training tailored for the various parties involved in the lifecycle of a payment: agency staff, beneficiaries, and service providers (when applicable).[42] The training for agency staff, for example, might emphasize methods for detecting improper payments, while training for beneficiaries and service providers might focus on program requirements.

In addition, GAO reiterated the need for agency managers to ensure that audit findings are resolved in a timely manner.[43] Managers have three important responsibilities in this regard,

---

[35] Ibid., p. 24.

[36] Office of Management and Budget, *Improper Payment Amounts Across the Federal Government (FYs 2004-2011)*, PaymentAccuracy.gov, at http://paymentaccuracy.gov.

[37] Government Accountability Office, *Improper Payments: Remaining Challenges and Strategies for Governmentwide Reduction Efforts*, GAO-12-573, March 2012, p. 11, at http://www.gao.gov/assets/590/589681.pdf.

[38] Ibid., p. 22.

[39] Ibid., p. 23.

[40] Ibid., p. 23.

[41] Ibid., p. 23.

[42] Ibid., p. 24.

[43] Ibid., p. 24.

according to GAO. First, they must promptly review any audit findings that show deficiencies in agency internal controls; second, they must determine the proper steps needed to resolve these deficiencies; and third, they must complete those steps within an established, expeditious time frame.[44]

Recovery Audits

One argument advanced by the proponents of IPERA was that it would increase the recovery of overpayments.[45] OMB issued government-wide guidance on the implementation of IPERA in April 2011. However, only about seven months of IPERA's payment recapture audit provisions were in effect by the time agencies reported on improper payments in their FY2011 Agency Financial Reports (AFRs).[46] That said, IPERA may have had a positive impact on efforts to recoup overpayments. According to the Treasury Department, agencies recaptured more than $1.2 billion in improper payments to contractors and vendors in FY2011,[47] which is nearly double the $688 million recaptured in FY2010.[48]

A recent GAO report noted that some agencies have indicated that statutory or regulatory barriers have interfered with their ability to perform recovery audits.[49] GAO identified the Office of Personnel Management (OPM) and the Department of Agriculture (USDA) as specific cases in point. In its FY2011 AFR, OPM stated that current law and Treasury Department regulations prohibit financial institutions from providing the requisite information to recover overpayments for its Retirement Program.[50] The USDA cited Section 281[51] of the Agriculture Reorganization Act of 1994[52] as the chief impediment to conducting recovery audits for the Farm Service Agency

---

[44] Ibid., p. 24.

[45] For example, see Sen. Thomas Carper, remarks in the Senate, *Congressional Record*, vol. 156, part 104 (July 14, 2010), p. S5809.

[46] For example, the Department of the Treasury's FY2011 AFR noted, "Due to the delayed release of IPERA implementation guidance, Treasury's bureaus were not able to fully implement or develop the mechanisms to acquire the additional information specified in the amended Payment Recapture Audit guidance." Department of the Treasury, *Agency Financial Report, Fiscal Year 2011*, November 15, 2011, p. 161, http://www.treasury.gov/about/budget-performance/annual-performance-plan/Documents/FY 2011 AFR-Final Version.pdf. OMB provided interim guidance on November 16, 2010. See OMB, "Increasing Efforts to Recapture Improper Payments by Intensifying and Expanding Payment Recapture Audits," Memorandum for Heads of Executive Departments and Agencies from Danny Werfel and Daniel I. Gordon, November 16, 2010, M-11-04.

[47] Department of the Treasury, *2011 Financial Report of the United States Government*, December 2011, at http://www.fms.treas.gov/fr/11frusg/11frusg.pdf.

[48] Office of Management and Budget, *Government-wide Improper Payments Recaptured (Billions)*, Performance.gov, at http://finance.performance.gov/content/initiative-recapture-improper-payments-508. According to PaymentAccuracy.gov, the increase from FY2010 to FY2011 is over 80%. See Office of Management and Budget, *About Improper Payments*, PaymentAccuracy.gov, at http://www.paymentaccuracy.gov.

[49] Government Accountability Office, *Improper Payments: Remaining Challenges and Strategies for Governmentwide Reduction Efforts*, GAO-12-573T, March 28, 2012, at http://www.gao.gov/assets/590/589681.pdf.

[50] The Social Security Administration (SSA), the Railroad Retirement Board (RRB), and the Department of Veterans Affairs (VA) are exempted from these restrictions, as specified in law. Office of Personnel Management, *Agency Financial Report, Fiscal Year 2011*, November 2011, at http://www.opm.gov/gpra/opmgpra/2011_AFR.pdf.

[51] According to the Department of Agriculture, "[T]his statute is commonly referred to as the 'Finality Rule'." Department of Agriculture, *Department of Agriculture's Consolidated Financial Statements for Fiscal Years 2011 and 2010*, November 2011, p. 220, at http://www.usda.gov/oig/webdocs/50401-0001-11.pdf.

[52] P.L. 103-354; 108 Stat. 3209.

(FSA) and Commodity Credit Corporation (CCC). Section 281 prohibits the recovery of incorrect payments after 90 days unless the participant believes the decision to be erroneous.[53]

Other agencies not cited in the GAO report have encountered problems, as well. The Department of Housing and Urban Development (HUD) explained that certain programs lack "the means to capture and report the amounts of improper payments identified and recovered."[54] The Department of Education (ED) cited the high burden of proof required to recover funds under the General Education Provisions Act (GEPA) as a barrier to recovery auditing.[55]

IPERA's cost-effectiveness requirement may limit the funds recovered through recovery audits. Under the law, agencies are required to conduct recovery audits only if so doing is cost-effective. If an agency determines that a recovery audit would not be cost-effective, it must notify the Office of Management and Budget (OMB) and its inspector general with the analysis it performed to reach this decision.

For FY2011, several agencies determined that recovery audits would not be cost-effective; two selected examples include the Treasury Department and the Small Business Administration (SBA). According to the Department of the Treasury's Office of Inspector General (OIG), neither the Treasury Executive Office for Asset Forfeiture (TEOAF) nor the Bureau of the Public Debt's Office of Public Debt Accounting (OPDA) performed recovery audits. The Treasury Department considered them low risk and immaterial and so deemed that recovery audits would not be cost-effective.[56] SBA cited low error rates and program complexity as reasons that payment audits would not be cost-effective. With regard to contracting specifically, for example, SBA stated that contracting's limited amount of outlays—$133.4 million over the improper payment period—meant that recovery audits would not be cost-effective.[57] Given that $133.4 million exceeded the $1 million threshold for conducting recovery audits under IPERA, SBA was required to provide a justification for this decision, but it did not.[58]

While OMB Circular A-123, Appendix C, instructs agencies on considerations they should take into account when evaluating whether a recovery audit would be cost-effective, there are no clear-cut criteria that would achieve a uniform response across agencies. Agency "opt-out" in the absence of definitive standards of cost-effectiveness could result in missed opportunities to recoup overpayments. In addition, understating amounts potentially available for recovery could

---

[53] Department of Agriculture, *Department of Agriculture's Consolidated Financial Statements for Fiscal Years 2011 and 2010*, November 2011, at http://www.usda.gov/oig/webdocs/50401-0001-11.pdf.

[54] Department of Housing and Urban Development, *Agency Financial Report, Fiscal Year 2011*, November 15, 2011, p. 182, at http://portal.hud.gov/huddoc/AFR2011.pdf.

[55] Department of Education, *FY 2011 Agency Financial Report*, November 15, 2011, at http://www2.ed.gov/about/reports/annual/2011report/agency-financial-report.pdf.

[56] Nor did Treasury notify OMB or its OIG. The OIG report notes that the materiality threshold is not up to the agency and that notification is required for all programs with expenditures of at least $1 million regardless of the agency's opinion on materiality. Office of Inspector General, Department of the Treasury, *Audit Report: Treasury Was Not in Compliance With IPERA for Fiscal Year 2011 (OIG-12-044)*, March 15, 2012, p. 6, at http://www.treasury.gov/about/organizational-structure/ig/Agency Documents/OIG12044 (web copy).pdf.

[57] Small Business Administration, *Agency Financial Report, Fiscal Year 2011*, November 15, 2011, at http://www.sba.gov/sites/default/files/Agency Financial Report FY 2011_0.pdf.

[58] Office of Inspector General, Small Business Administration, Advisory Memorandum: The SBA's Improper Payment Review and Reporting for its Contracting Activities did not Comply with IPERA and IPIA Requirements During FY 2011 (Report No. 12-07), March 8, 2012, at http://www.sba.gov/sites/default/files/Report 12-07 IPERA and IPIA review.pdf.

---

limit congressional oversight, as incomplete and incorrect information might impede effective program monitoring and review.

Legislation in the 112th Congress

S. 1409, the Improper Payments Elimination and Recovery Improvement Act (IPERIA), was introduced on July 22, 2011, reported favorably by the Senate Committee on Homeland Security and Government Affairs on July 12, 2012, and passed the Senate with an amendment by unanimous consent on August 1, 2012. S. 1409 was then sent to the House and referred to the Committee on Oversight and Government Reform (COGR). The House passed a companion version of the bill, H.R. 4053, the Improper Payments Elimination and Recovery Improvement Act of 2012, on December 13, 2012, by a vote of 402-0, and the bill was received in the Senate on December 17, 2012.[59]

Improper Payments

IPERIA would require OMB to identify a list of "high-priority" federal programs for greater levels of oversight. These programs would be chosen on the basis of the relatively high dollar value or error rate of improper payments, or because they are deemed more susceptible to improper payments when compared to other high-risk programs, regardless of size. OMB would be required to establish annual targets, as well as quarterly and semi-annual actions for reducing improper payments for the high-priority programs. In addition, each agency with a high-priority program would be required to submit an annually report on the steps agencies have taken, and plan to take, to prevent and recover future improper payments. The report would be submitted to the inspector general of the agency and posted on a website accessible to the public. The inspector general, in turn, would be required to submit a report to Congress that assesses the quality of the improper payment estimates for each high-priority program, determines whether proper controls are in place to identify and prevent future improper payments, and makes recommendations to Congress on how agency plans might be modified to improve their improper payment estimates and internal controls.

IPERIA would also require OMB to issue new guidance intended to increase the accuracy of agency improper payment estimates. The bill would establish new standards for sampling payments, bar agencies from relying on self-reporting of recipients for estimates, require agencies to include all improper payments in its estimates—including those payments recovered or in the process of being recovered—and include payments to employees in their estimates.

IPERIA would require a "Do Not Pay Initiative" similar to the "Do Not Pay List" established by President Barack Obama.[60] Under IPERIA, agencies would be required to verify recipient

---

[59] H.R. 4053 is similar, but not identical to, S. 1409—there are some technical details regarding the process by which agencies share data. The discussion of IPERA above is limited to major provisions that are shared by both the House and Senate version of the bill. H.R. 4053, as amended, may be found at http://www.gpo.gov/fdsys/pkg/BILLS-112hr4053rh/pdf/BILLS-112hr4053rh.pdf.

[60] The "Do Not Pay List" is a network of databases that contain information on a recipient's eligibility to receive federal benefits payments or federal awards, such as grants and contracts. Barack Obama, "Presidential Memorandum—Enhancing Payment Accuracy Through a 'Do Not Pay List,'" June 18, 2010, at http://www.whitehouse.gov/the-press-office/presidential-memorandum-enhancing-payment-accuracy-through-a-do- (continued...)

---

eligibility by reviewing available databases prior to issuing a payment or award. At a minimum, agencies would be required to verify eligibility by reviewing data in the

- Death Master File, maintained by the Social Security Administration;
- Excluded Parties List System, maintained by the General Services Administration;
- Debt Check Database, maintained by the Department of the Treasury;
- Credit Alert System, maintained by the Department of Housing and Urban Development; and
- List of Excluded Parties and Entities, maintained by the inspector general of the Department of Health and Human Services.

OMB would have the authority to include additional databases as part of the "Do Not Pay Initiative," as long as the public was provided notice and opportunity to comment before the database would be included. OMB would be required to ensure that the "Do Not Pay Initiative" is established at each agency and to report on the initiative's usefulness each year.

In addition to drawing on data from existing sources, IPERIA would require the Attorney General to submit a report to Congress within a year from enactment that would assess the ability of using state, local, and Federal incarceration status as a method for identifying and preventing improper payments. IPERIA would also require the Social Security Administration (SSA) to take steps to improve the accuracy and timeliness of death data maintained by SSA.

Recovery Audits

Under IPERA, agencies must establish annual payment recapture targets for their programs. By FY2013, the proportion of recovered amounts to amounts identified for recovery must be at least 0.85 (that is, a recovery rate of at least 85%). S. 1409 would expand upon these provisions by requiring the Director of OMB to set recovery targets for improper payments, with specific amounts identified for recovery audit contractors. In addition, the legislation would require the Director of OMB to determine both current and historical improper payments recovery amounts and rates, including those recaptured by recovery audit contractors, and provide a list of agency recovery audit contract programs.[61]

Concluding Observations on IPERIA

IPERIA's provisions target areas for improvement that are known to be weak, particularly with regard to developing more accurate improper payment estimates. In addition, the explicit requirement to include payments to federal employees when estimating improper payments may yield new areas for savings, as OMB has reported that federal benefit programs may be

---

(...continued)

not-pay-list.

[61] Agencies report current-year information on recaptured amounts and rates, as well as cumulative recoveries, in their AFRs. A-123 requires agencies to separate reportable information resulting from internal recovery audits from that uncovered by recovery audit contractors.

susceptible to high rates of improper payments—perhaps over $1 billion a year. In FY2008, for example, the Office of Personnel Management reported more than $330 million in improper payments for federal health, life, and retirement programs,[62] and the Department of Defense reported more than $730 million in improper payments for military and civilian pay, health, and retirement programs.[63] Finally, the ability of agencies to access data from a range of sources across the government may prove to be a valuable tool for preventing payments to ineligible recipients. The cost of integrating and improving existing data sources as IPERIA envisions, however, should be compared to the potential savings generated by doing so.

Author Contact Information

Garrett Hatch
Specialist in American National Government
ghatch@crs.loc.gov, 7-7822

Meredith A. Levine
Analyst in Government Organization and Management
mlevine@crs.loc.gov, 7-8417

---

[62] Office of Personnel Management, *Agency Financial Report, Fiscal Year 2008*, November 17, 2008, p. 134, at http://www.opm.gov/gpra/opmgpra/par2008/par2008.pdf.

[63] Department of Defense, *Fiscal Year 2008 Agency Financial Report*, November 17, 2008, p. 133, at http://comptroller.defense.gov/afr/fy2008/
Fiscal_Year_2008_Department_of_Defense_Agency_Wide_Financial_Statements_and_Notes.pdf.

www.ingramcontent.com/pod-product-compliance
Lightning Source LLC
Chambersburg PA
CBHW080811290526
45790CB00008B/3663